D0604289

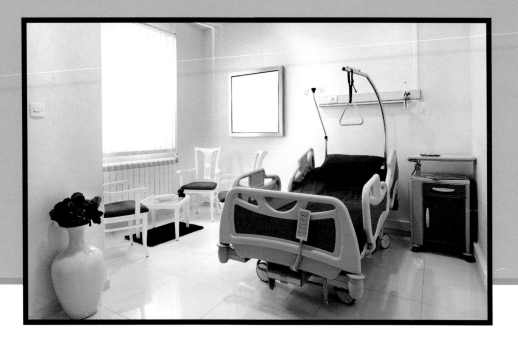

Community Helpers at the Hospital

by Mari Schuh

CAPSTONE PRESS
a capstone imprint

Little Pebble is published by Capstone Press,
1710 Roe Crest Drive, North Mankato, Minnesota 56003
www.mycapstone.com

Library of Congress Cataloging-in-Publication Data
Names: Schuh, Mari C., 1975– author.
Title: Community helpers at the hospital / by Mari Schuh.
Description: North Mankato, Minnesota : Little Pebble Books, an imprint of
Capstone Press, [2017] | Series: Little pebble. Community helpers on the
scene | Audience: Ages 4–8. | Audience: K to grade 3. | Includes
bibliographical references and index.
Identifiers: LCCN 2016009758| ISBN 9781515723974 (library binding) | ISBN
9781515724087 (pbk.) | ISBN 9781515724148 (ebook (pdf))
Subjects: LCSH: Hospitals—Juvenile literature. | Hospitals—Employees—Juvenile literature. |
Medical care—Juvenile literature.
Classification: LCC RA963.5 .S38 2017 | DDC 362.11—dc23
LC record available at http://lccn.loc.gov/2016009758

Editorial Credits
Megan Atwood, editor; Juliette Peters, designer;
Pam Mitsakos, media researcher; Tori Abraham, production specialist

Photo Credits
Alamy Images: Blend Images, 10-11, Vstock, 15; Getty Images: B Busco, 6-7, Marc Romanelli,
16-17; Glow Images: Juice Images, 20-21; Shutterstock: A and N photography, 18-19,
bikeriderlondon, 9, Dxinerz-Pvt-Ltd, 3, 24, back cover, Marko Poplasen, 1, Spotmatik Ltd, 4-5,
wavebreakmedia, cover, xmee, 12-13

Printed in the United States of America in North Mankato, Minnesota.
009674F16

Table of Contents

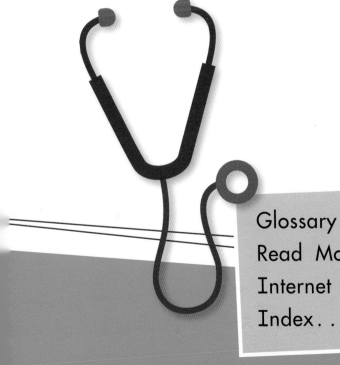

Getting Well

Joe is sick.

Lia is hurt.

Who helps people
at the hospital?

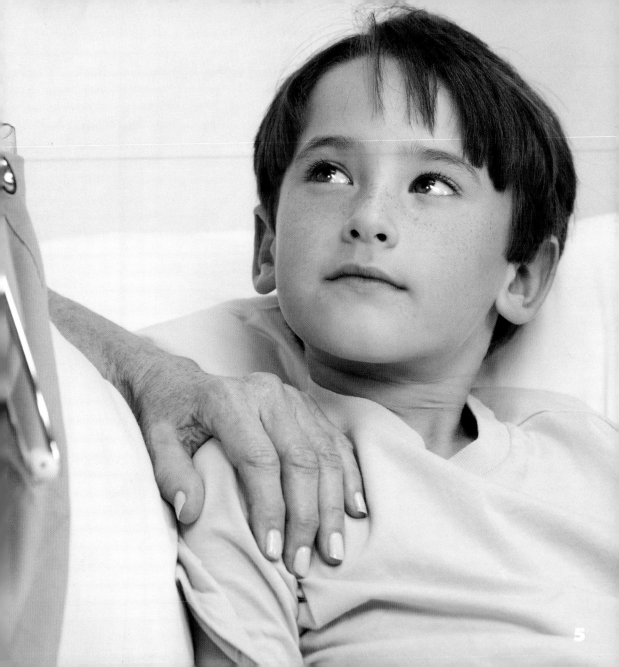

So Many Helpers

Cy broke his arm.

It hurts.

Cy sees a doctor.

She orders an X-ray.

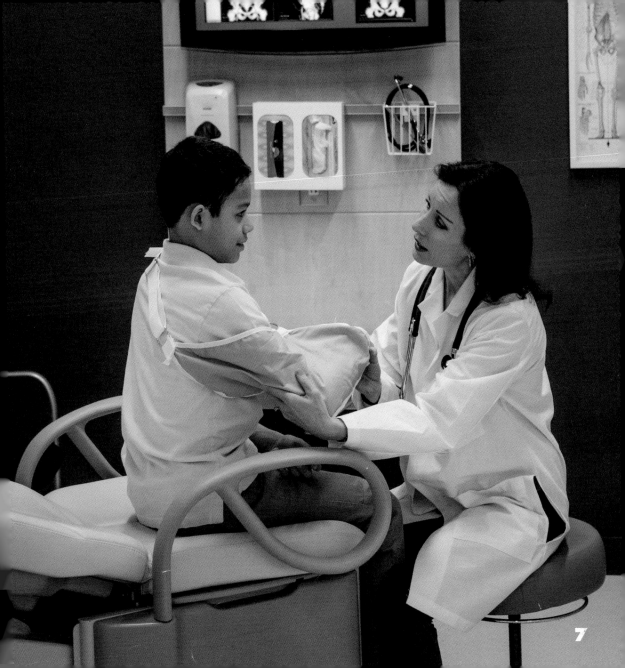

Ike is well.

He has a check-up.

A nurse weighs him.

Mae needs pills.

A pharmacist gets

the pills ready.

All set!

Oh, no. Not again.

Cole's tonsils hurt.

A surgeon takes them out.

Get well soon!

A volunteer runs
the gift shop.
Eli buys a toy.

Al is upset.

He talks to a counselor.

She helps him.

Is Kim sick?

A lab worker runs tests.

Good news!

Kim is ok.

Many helpers work

at a hospital.

They help people get well.

Glossary

counselor—a person who is trained to help people during hard times

doctor—a person who treats sick and hurt people

nurse—a person who cares for sick and hurt people

pharmacist—a person who gets medicine ready for people

surgeon—a doctor who does surgeries on people

volunteer—a person who does a job without being paid

Read More

Keogh, Josie. *A Trip to the Hospital.* My Community. New York: PowerKids Press, 2013.

Murray, Julie. *Nurses.* Going to Work. Edina, Minn.: ABDO Publishing, 2011.

Rissman, Rebecca. *Going to the Doctor.* Comparing Past and Present. Chicago: Capstone Heinemann Library, 2014.

Internet Sites

FactHound offers a safe, fun way to find Internet sites related to this book. All of the sites on FactHound have been researched by our staff.

Here's all you do:
Visit *www.facthound.com*
Type in this code: 9781515723974

Check out projects, games and lots more at
www.capstonekids.com

Index

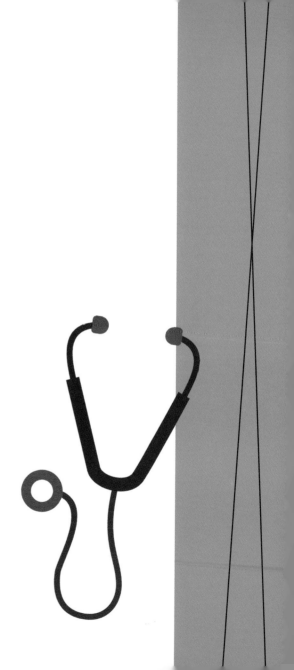